THE
CREATIVE **HOME**

THE
CREATIVE HOME
INSPIRING IDEAS FOR BEAUTIFUL LIVING

Geraldine James

CICO BOOKS
LONDON NEW YORK

Published in 2016 by CICO Books
An imprint of Ryland Peters & Small Ltd
20–21 Jockey's Fields   341 E 116th St
London WC1R 4BW   New York, NY 10029

www.rylandpeters.com

10 9 8 7 6 5 4 3 2 1

A CIP catalog record for this book is available from
the Library of Congress and the British Library.

ISBN: 978-1-78249-358-7

Printed in China

Images and text were previously published in *Creative
Walls*, *Creative Display*, and *Creative Spaces*, all published
by CICO Books

Cover designer and design concept: Paul Tilby
Photographer: Andrew Wood
(pages 16, 17, 50, 51, 52, 53, 82, 106, 107, 114,
115, 238, 239, and cover spine by Rick Haylor;
page 201 by Jude Morgan)

Senior editor: Carmel Edmonds
In-house designer: Fahema Khanam
Art director: Sally Powell
Production manager: Gordana Simakovic
Publishing manager: Penny Craig
Publisher: Cindy Richards

CONTENTS

INTRODUCTION 6

CHAPTER 1 COOK & EAT   8

CHAPTER 2 RELAX & SOCIALIZE   66

CHAPTER 3 WORK & CREATE   110

CHAPTER 4: SLEEP & BATHE   144

CHAPTER 5 STORE & DISPLAY   202

INDEX 254

PICTURE CREDITS 256

INTRODUCTION

In my day-to-day role as an interior buyer, and equally in my personal life, visiting the homes of friends, I have concluded that style is a completely personal thing—you just have to be confident in letting it shine in your home. Whether you have magpie-like tendencies and cherished collections, or you prefer clear surfaces and a minimalist look, the important thing is to believe in your choices. Keep a few basic design principles in mind, certainly—but then go for it.

This book features snapshots from a huge variety of homes, from period properties to modern apartments, and often you'll find that within even a single room different periods and styles are mixed together to great effect. These homeowners have considered focus, proportion, and functionality, but have always kept at the heart of their design what makes their house feel like home.

There are four chapters on different rooms and areas of the house—Cook and Eat features kitchens and dining spaces, Relax and Socialize covers living rooms, Work and Create includes home offices and studios, and Sleep and Bathe, of course, shows bedrooms and bathrooms. The final chapter, Store and Display, shows how different areas of the home can be used to show off your treasures and store your collections.

I hope you will be inspired by these ideas, no matter how big or small, new or old your own home may be. Experiment with color, materials, and arrangements, until what you see is a true reflection of you and what you love.

CHAPTER I
COOK & EAT

CREATIVE KITCHENS

While it is one of the most functional rooms of the house, the kitchen does not have to be without style; indeed, it is all the more important to inject your own character into this area, as it is one that you will most likely spend time in every day.

The owner of this house has a love of raw wood, and it is very much in evidence in this bespoke kitchen. The cabinets have all been treated with a dark stain, which gives a really earthy quality, but the kitchen still has all the trappings of an efficient workspace. Patterned glazed tiles make a pretty splashback behind the modern, stainless-steel stove. The shelves not only provide extra storage, but also a space to display different types of stoneware that the owner has collected.

Left This open-plan kitchen opens out onto the garden, which, along with the raw wooden cabinets, potted plants above the sink, and fresh flowers on the table, gives a real feel of bringing nature into the home.

Above left Above the kitchen work surface hangs a rather bold abstract painting by one of the owners. The brushed steel appliances are an incongruous but fitting match with this striking piece of art.

Right In spite of hectic schedules, care is always taken over presentation. Set for breakfast, the well-dressed kitchen table displays a delectable feast, with elegant cakestands for cheese and fruit, matching mugs of coffee, and various holders for the boiled eggs.

Below left To the left of the stove, a small silver pitcher of flowers and a pretty table lamp, presided over by another abstract painting by one of the owners, show how a functional kitchen can also be decorative.

A well-designed, modern kitchen sits alongside the art created by its owners

These three pictures are of the same kitchen in the home just outside Paris of two artists and their children. It comes as no surprise that the couple's paintings are hanging throughout the house. Even the kitchen highlights their creative energy and artistic vision. But the room is much more than a picture gallery. For such a busy couple, it is especially important for the kitchen to be practical and to work efficiently, but it must also be comfortable and aesthetically pleasing. This they have achieved apparently without effort, neatly combining function with art. Three crystal-drop chandeliers hanging over the table provide the unexpected finishing touches, combined with the beautiful French linen.

Design meets function in this dazzling French country kitchen

Above Two dark green enamel lamp shades hang low over the dining table, their color suiting the rustic style of the kitchen. A generous vase of flowers, picked from the garden, adds just the right decorative touch. The windows have been thrown open to let the early fall sun stream through and bring life to this glorious space.

Right A row of pots and pans hanging from the wall, a large stew pot, and a set of weighing scales are all neatly stored in this compact and functional space, to make life easier for the cook.

In this home near Paris, we witness a wonderful example of design and decoration. The owner has made her kitchen, that most functional of rooms, a pleasure to be in and a place to linger. Thinking first and foremost of her family, who will sit down to enjoy their meals, she has given center stage to the large wooden table.

A grand old clock hangs above a side table, decorative as well as practical, as are the cast-iron dish beneath, the lamp, and the collection of dishes and bowls, all ready to be used. The highchair set at one end of the table welcomes a small grandchild to join the adults. Everything here has been put together with a subtle and sympathetic eye, totally in keeping with the traditional charm of the house.

The room seen below, just off the main kitchen, was once the food and cooking store. Now, it provides a home for the pots and pans, hung from metal hooks above the old shallow stone sink, and useful storage for fruit and vegetables brought in fresh from the local market.

Left The suspended white cabinet hanging over the stove is the perfect platform for this collection of worn vintage numbers painted onto tin. Beneath is a clock leaning on the chalkboard. The whole scene is casual but cohesive.

Above These white-painted numbers most certainly had a functional purpose in their previous life on the scoreboard of an Australian cricket pavilion, and there is even a hole in the tin for hanging them. Their reincarnation in this kitchen as leaning art is inspired.

How intriguing is this picture! In an ultra-modern functional kitchen, a whole group of vintage numbers painted onto tin has been propped up against a textured chalkboard wall above a pure white suspended cabinet.

The owner has a real love of monochrome—the theme of the whole apartment is black and white—and it was extremely clever of him to visualize these numbers in such an environment, where they give a unique twist to an otherwise functional space. When he came across them at an antiques fair, he knew instinctively that they would work really well in his home. Leaning gives you the opportunity to experiment—for the present, the numbers are in the kitchen but they could easily be moved elsewhere to take on a completely different look. The numbers appear to have been placed quite randomly here but one never knows!

The kitchen can still provide a place to display your collections. Two views of the same kitchen show a selection of intriguing objects, including a posy of teddy bear glass eyes, hanging from hooks, creating an eclectic piece of wall art. The vintage brushed steel plate rack is attractive as well as practical.

A selection of unique objects in
white creates a stunning impact.
Even everyday kitchen items look
special when grouped together
and displayed with care.

CREATIVE DINING

Dining areas provide the perfect opportunity to explore different table settings, whether you host dinner parties or informal gatherings with friends, or whether it's a space for the inhabitants of the house to come to eat and spend time together.

The decorating style in this house is about creating comfort and warmth against a blank canvas. With no competing colors and textures to contend with, the displays can be easily changed and the spaces re-invented with new pieces of art. For a sophisticated affair, as shown here, vintage glassware and plain white plates decorate a white linen tablecloth, so that the setting resembles something like a Dutch 17th-century still-life oil painting. However, the owners of the house like to cook and experiment with different cuisines, so when serving colorful, spicy cuisine, out come the bright plates, tablecloth, and napkins; the dining experience takes on a completely different guise.

Right Even though this long table is set for an informal lunch, it has been laid with care, using a French linen tablecloth, albeit unironed, a selection of vintage carafes and decanters, white linen napkins, and silver cutlery. An oil painting of an embroidered dress by one of the owners hangs on the wall. Making an unlikely but perfect match are the clay pigeon and white ceramic pitcher on the window ledge.

Right and below Many languid hours are spent at this kitchen table in the south of France, eating and chatting in the utmost comfort, not to mention style. This is the hub of the home, and the kitchen has been designed with that in mind—there is no need for a separate dining room. The upholstered sofa, bench, and armchairs invite relaxation, so that no one feels inclined to move. Covered in a crisp white tablecloth, with off-white china and bone-handled cutlery, all ready for breakfast, the table is perfectly balanced with the soft green Paisley design of the upholstery and the duck-egg-blue of the paintwork. The look is altogether soothing and fresh.

Next page In the same French kitchen, lunch is about to be served. The approach to the display is slightly different here. Instead of being covered with a cloth, the bronze tabletop has been left bare, highlighting the pale turquoise plates perfectly.

Left An old mirror, with foxing adding to its charm, is propped up on the painted chest of drawers. The art and vintage finds share a common finish of white and aged patina, uniting the display. A limited edition print of Tracey Emin's "Walking Around My World" hangs above the mirror. Equally precious are the photograph and drawing by Richard Nott and a porcelain tureen decorated with hand-molded roses on the lid.

Above Leaning against the white wall, on top of a long, dark gray console table, is another old mirror. This forms the backdrop to an informal display of a white hydrangea in a beautifully aged plant pot, a glass vase of contorted twigs, and a French crystal-drop light.

Right The glass-fronted cabinet is both handsome and functional, housing all my glassware and china. Adding a note of glamour above the table, which is set for a simple afternoon tea, is an antique French crystal chandelier.

This is the dining room from my own apartment. Previously, I was known for having white in my home, but I have recently embraced color—or at least shades of gray. The floors throughout the apartment are now painted a dark gray, and I'm really pleased with the result—it somehow pulls the apartment together. I dyed the dining tablecloth to match and changed all the wall art—which appears in this room (see above), as well as elsewhere—to white.

Above A simple table setting on this raw wood table extends a compelling invitation to dine. Both the table and the benches are made of recycled wood from water towers. Black metal-mesh chairs by Russell Woodard supplement the seating. The oil painting to the right is by friend and artist Rainer Andreesen, and depicts the owner's father in the late 1930s.

Right Each piece on this table is decorative as well as practical. The white china and small glass plates, the vintage crystal pot of preserves, and the stack of white linen napkins tied with string look striking against the raw table. Nature plays a part, too, with a dried hydrangea and a huge chunk of wood used as a bread container.

Meticulous attention to detail makes dining in this space very special

Above A focused selection of decorative objects—an ornate Victorian tureen, with molded ceramic flowers on the lid, glass domes of varying sizes containing ceramic birds, and a carved marble cross—gathered on top of the small console table in the dining room creates a well-balanced display. Hanging above the table is a moody etching by Andrew Dalton.

The fresh, bright appeal of this dining room comes from the sleek and consistent styling, and the focus on brilliant white paintwork. The owner is extremely creative, and has a natural ability to devise simple and clever decorating ideas. She has collected many retro vases and objects, which she has skillfully sprayed in matte black or white paint, creating striking monochrome vignettes, to give the room a focused look. Presentation is of utmost importance. When setting the table, for example, she takes great care with the overall look and color balance.

This is the dining room from the previous page seen at a different angle, looking from the kitchen. In this pared-down space, the vintage white French armoire, home to all the beautiful ceramics and sets of china, catches the eye, its beveled mirror front reflecting the white Venetian blinds. In direct contrast, the table is set with black accessories, creating a more dramatic effect as the natural light fades and the hanging industrial lamp in the corner gives a warm glow.

This large through-room is the focal point for family dining as well as entertaining. The vintage brushed-steel table, chairs, and glazed cabinet give an urban, industrial feel, but this is offset by the ceramic pitcher of flowers and glassware, creating a distinctive yet relaxed dining area. The beautiful parquet floors are original to the house and also help to soften the space. On the opposite side of the room is the marble fireplace, also original, with various decorative objects jostling for space on top.

Left A brushed-steel table and matching curved-back chairs, which might once have belonged in a small factory or office, now have pride of place in this contemporary home. Vinyl-coated vintage office chairs introduce a softer and eclectic feel to this cool and sophisticated space.

Next page When you enter this beachside house in Malibu, you are immediately struck by its simple, relaxed beauty. The look appears effortless but that is the deception. Great care has been taken to choose pieces of furniture with a worn patina or subtle colors, soft worn linen tablecloths, and mismatched vintage glasses and china. Together, items that have had a previous life go to make up a home with a heart.

Left The relaxed atmosphere at this informal supper has been easily achieved with the casual mismatch of candlesticks, glasses, and chairs. As the light fades, the room takes on a romantic atmosphere. Flickering candlelight reflected in the crystal chandelier adds to the magic of the display, while flowers placed in a ceramic pitcher are the perfect finishing touch.

Above Humor is the order of the day with this table display. In shades of orange, this "vegetarian banquet," complete with a chunky ceramic rabbit that has various body parts molded as vegetables, would put a smile on anyone's face!

Next page Glassware gives added elegance to this softly lit dining room of muted tones, with the twinkling candlesticks and chandelier helping to create a strong and dramatic atmosphere. Reflecting it all is the handsome antique mirror at one end of the room.

The wooden folding screen, painted by a contemporary Japanese artist, establishes the predominantly oriental feel of this dining space. Unusual japanned Queen Anne chairs flank the chunky, white-lacquered dining table, where the owner is about to take tea served from a 1960s Spode teapot. Pink roses in a glass vase inject color and give balance to this graphic setting.

This long wooden dining table is found within an open-plan kitchen, part of a modern and well-organized home. A long cabinet fits against the wall, its open shelves housing neatly stacked piles of the family's everyday china. Hidden behind the sliding doors are less attractive kitchen essentials. The large pieces of art are by the owner and his son. They make up what appears to be a casual display but, together with the carved mask protected under a glass dome and the unusual candlesticks, it is, in fact, meticulously thought-out and arranged. The table, complemented by white Saarinen chairs, is perfect for family meals as well as entertaining. A single lily in a vase is all that's needed to dress the space.

White walls and paintwork work well with the soft tones of the wooden dining table and the trim on the cabinets. White, industrial-style uplights are evenly spaced on either side.

COKI

Using white as the overall theme has given a purity to this dining space, making it striking, calm, and very relaxing. The gentle curves of the large oval table and the chairs, both design classics, suit the space and the owners' aesthetic perfectly. The still-life painting in neutral tones injects warmth, as do the chair cushions and tiled floor.

Chosen both for its beauty and warm tones, the custom-made dining table by Peter Alexander at the heart of this LA home, left, is made of solid maple with a sycamore veneer. In complementary tones are the Tom Charnock chairs, with cashmere covers. The striking piece of art, reminiscent of a triptych, is by Russian painter Timur D'Vatz. Illuminating the scene is a modern take on a chandelier in bronzed steel.

When you peer through the archway in the 1920s Californian apartment in the picture on the right, you are met with a delightful, personal scene. Warm yellow walls set off the plain dining table and chairs. The owner sits here to have his meals, as well as do some daily tasks. The colors and mixed cultures represented in the room are indicative of his style and interests.

The owners of both these homes are true to their individual styles. The rooms have different cultural references, but are striking for their bold color choice and decoration. I love the fact that they both proclaim their unique and carefully thought-out design.

Below This harmonious display of objects from different cultures and in varied styles is bathed in a gentle, filtered light.

Left Like everything else in this room, the tulips have been chosen with great care and thought, and are the absolutely perfect color match.

Every aspect of this sophisticated room is testament to the skill and good judgment of its owners. It is disciplined and ordered, with nothing ill considered or out of place. To achieve such a well-balanced display of stunning art and photography, all the pieces were first laid out on the floor and moved around until the perfect composition was achieved. You can see the striking opposite wall of this room on pages 104–105.

Above and above right The colored panels of this Plexiglas table can be interchanged to vary the color combination and composition, as well as the kaleidoscopic effects on the surrounding walls.

Right This black walnut dining table is twenty-six feet long with a ten-foot dining section. Red-upholstered chairs complement the space well and ensure complete comfort in this family home.

These photographs are of two modern loft spaces in different New York homes, where tables are the immediate focus of attention. The Plexiglas table featured above has been designed by Jonny Detiger for his own home. It is an intriguing piece but also practical, with many family meals held around it. Light enters the apartment at different angles throughout the day and, while passing through the Plexiglas, it projects a kaleidoscope of rays onto the walls, bringing about subtle color changes to the room.

In the dining room seen on the left, a remarkable walnut table designed by US-based Chinese architect David Ling is the center of attention. Twenty-six feet long, this ten-foot dining section serves as the multifunctional hub of the home. Used for meals, homework, school projects, or simply surfing the internet, it is quite simply the family workhorse and a perfect example of how good design can satisfy the practical needs of a family.

A love of 20th-century style and design is evident here with the marble-topped dining table and classic Charles and Ray Eames chairs, in aluminum and leather as well as molded plastic. Softening the space are a cowhide rug and a neutral-colored Scandinavian woolen rug in the adjoining seating area. Above the leather Cappellini sofa hangs an Andy Warhol print, the reflected strips of another set of Venetian blinds scoring the face of this 1960s icon.

outdoor dining

In warmer weather, eating outside can be a particular pleasure. While the outdoors alone creates a wonderful atmosphere, a little styling can add to this, continuning the theme of the interiors.

Water provides the setting and spectacular backdrop for this beach setting. The aim of the outdoor breakfast table in Malibu is to relax in style and enjoy being by the sea. As this picture shows, this has been achieved beyond any reasonable doubt and by the simplest means. What better place to enjoy a leisurely weekend breakfast, or to watch the sun go down over the horizon? Blue and white always make perfect partners, and here an undemanding table setting of well laundered and softly crumpled chair covers and tablecloth and mismatched vintage tableware enhances rather than detracts from the expanse of clear blue sea seen beyond the vast picture windows.

Right A white tablecloth and slipcovers introduce a touch of elegance to this relaxing outdoor breakfast at this beachside house in Malibu. The warm Californian sun filters through the lattice roof, while the ocean provides breathtaking scenery.

Left This outbuilding provides a space for informal dining with an outdoor feel, while remaining under cover. The top of the Ercole table is inlaid with mosaic tiles, and its spindly metal legs complement those of the chairs. This area is also used for storage, housing logs for the fire and gardening tools, but these become part of the decoration.

Above The painted metal wall sconce from Ercole has been made to look vintage. So very pretty, it holds two candles that will add a romantic glow to the space as the light fades. Sitting on the brick ledge above is a framed drawing of a coat of arms. When put together, these two distinctive and unconnected pieces create a beautiful yet simple display.

Left Modernism meets country in this uncluttered, tranquil space.

Above A weathered old table is dressed up for a special occasion. Garden flowers tied to the chair backs with string add to the rustic charm.

These two spaces in the same converted barn in France display the owners' love of mixed styles. The modernist table and chairs on the left are in stark contrast to the pale stone walls and pastoral feel of their setting. The other table, worn and unrefined, is set for a celebration lunch. Decorative touches, such as a candelabra, add to the sense of occasion.

Simple decorating styles allow the natural beauty of stone to shine through

Left The weathered table and bench form the foundations for this simple lunch, while the white, curlicue chairs provide the decoration and bring light into an otherwise quite gloomy space.

Above A white metal chair, a napkin cut from an old rice sack and lined with a white paper napkin, a pear on a small terracotta dish, a wicker-encased glass tumbler—all these elements combine perfectly at this quiet outdoor table setting.

Above right A delightful place card created from a pear tied with a luggage label around its stalk.

An old stone wall provides shelter and a solid backdrop for this plain lunch, in keeping with the unpainted wood of the seasoned table and bench. Although the elements that make up the table display, from terracotta and hemp to wicker and string, may be considered rough and unsophisticated, they are totally charming in this environment. In spite of the modesty of the scene, there is no doubt that great care has gone into its creation. And who could help but feel special when greeted by a handwritten place card tied with string around a pear?

A natural wall backdrop in this covered outdoor space is the perfect setting for a display of very pretty vintage plates that have been collected over the years. The plates are hung in no particular order, with some overlapping. Their soft colors complement the battered green bench and the old floral curtain, used here as a tablecloth.

Left and above Above the bench hangs a lovely display of vintage plates, united only by their similar tones.

Right The kitsch prints hanging together in the corner of this space make a particularly strong image when joined by old Lloyd Loom chairs.

CHAPTER 2

RELAX & SOCIALIZE

CREATIVE LIVING

These spaces for rest and relaxation come in a variety of styles—and as seen here, comfortable need not mean casual.

This room is part of an absolutely gorgeous Georgian house of immense architectural merit, where the owners live with their two children and Pucci, the Pomeranian. There was an incredible amount of restoration work to be done before the family was able to move in, but the result is a house restored to its former grandeur but at the same time it is a happy, relaxed space that the boisterous children enjoy, too, with nothing in it that is too precious to be touched.

Painted and decorated in various shades of white, as well as being light and airy, the space exudes peace and calm.

Left Except for the original dark-stained floorboards, this gracious and light-filled living room is an homage to white. Beautiful original paneled walls, a stunning marble fireplace, French doors opening out onto the garden—all these elements create a quiet serenity. Although modern, the long sofa, with a gray cashmere throw over one arm, is at perfect ease among all these impressive architectural features. Not to be outdone or overlooked, Pucci has placed herself center stage.

Next page This beautiful, long room is within the same house. At one end, narrow folding screens, which almost reach the ceiling, are covered in damask wallpaper offering a relief against the plain wall. With smart but comfortable upholstered furniture arranged symmetrically, tonal cushions, and arrangements of small white flowers on the coffee table, the look is streamlined, unfussy, and welcoming.

Above Like the other rooms, this living space has been decorated in subtle tones, but with the clever use of stronger colors in the yellow retro lamp and the lime-green cushion on the wool sofa. Once again, the juxtaposition of unlikely partners —the marble fireplace and the Saarinen Tulip table—is a success.

Right The bare brick walls give a real earthy look to this space, complementing the contemporary gilt mirror and neutral gray sofa.

Above, we see a renovated 20th-century Brooklyn brownstone provide a gorgeous historic backdrop to an exciting mix of contemporary furniture and furnishings. There is a subtle blend of styles, but with a lean toward the mid-20th century. White walls and paintwork have allowed the owners to be adventurous in their choices. The retro lamp by the window, with its acid-yellow base, was an enviable find at a vintage market—a real gem. A worn animal skin partly covers the original floorboards, while light is softly filtered through linen curtains.

The room on the right is found within a loft space in Borough, on the south side of the River Thames. The building was originally a school dating from 1910, and the apartment is in the section where boys were once taught. The simple stone fireplace is original.

Both of these living rooms showcase how original features can be combined with more modern pieces to great effect, as well displaying how muted colors can add warmth to an overall white interior.

Above Slatted shutters fill the bay windows of this comfortable living space, filtering light and allowing privacy. The matching antique chairs not only provide occasional seating, but become a feature in their own right, positioned in the bay window in this way.

Art is a quick and easy way to transform the feel of a space, as well as speaking volumes about its owner

Housed within another period property, this living space again shows how new and old, and neutrals and dark accents, can come together. Nothing is left to chance here: one of the owners is a retail interiors and textiles buyer, and has a very clear understanding of what she wants and, indeed, wants to live with, from the paint color for the walls to the finish of the floorboards. Her husband is a restaurant owner and an avid collector of street art and urban graphics, as is evidenced above. The two styles have been merged with great integrity: the home is warm and tranquil but with a sharp urban edge.

Above Two artworks on the wall—a Dran piece, "Monkey at Work," by the window, and the David Bailey photographic print, "King of Clubs"—hint at a more subversive, humorous approach to decoration than would otherwise be suggested by the modern, cream corner sofa unit, pouffe, and antique chairs.

All the ingredients for the perfect afternoon tea can be found in this cozy lounge. A gold teapot and elegant porcelain cups, together with a crystal cake stand and delicious creamy cakes, are laid out on a tray on top of a linen-covered ottoman. The reclining bronze of a woman is an indicator of how relaxed the atmosphere is, while the candlelight and the open fire provide just the right amount of light. And who could overlook Rikki the rescue dog?

Left The unusual occasional table in this sunny reading corner complements the stone floor and the warm colors of the chaise longue.

Right A vintage coffee table adds a real sense of individualism to this space, while the soft gray linen sofa and decorative screen make a harmonious backdrop.

Far right The eye is immediately drawn to this exquisite decorative lamp in etched glass on top of a Chinese lacquered wooden table.

Below A weathered metal garden table has been brought indoors as an informal surface for displaying candles, flowers, and a treasured collection of shells and coral.

occasional tables

Placed next to an armchair or in front of a sofa, occasional tables can be used to hold a lamp, place a hot drink, rest a book, show off a cherished object. Here are some great examples of different styles of table, how they can be used, and how they become a focal point in the room.

In the picture opposite, beside the chaise longue, is a very unusual occasional table. Resembling a large barrel with a metal stand on top to hold the glass, it is a decorative item in its own right. The two bowls on the table do not compete but simply reflect the carefully balanced color scheme of the room. Conversely, if an item is of sufficient beauty, then it deserves to be the focus of attention. In the picture above, a stunning etched glass lamp draws the eye.

Bear in mind that occasional tables need not always be designed specifically for the role. Provided it is flat and stable, almost anything can be used as a showcase for a variety of displays.

Left This young
designer's home is
a showcase of his
creative skills.
A discarded vinyl LP
has been re-invented
as the top of a side
table, while an old
cine camera has been
adapted to become
a desk lamp. Clever,
inventive, and, above
all, stylish.

Right These bellows
from a foundry have
needed no adaptation
to take on a different
but still practical role
as a coffee table. Their
dark, rich leather sits
comfortably with the
modern, upholstered
sofa, and they give
the room a truly
individual look.

Left and above A disused packing crate has been adapted for use as a coffee table, and now makes a wonderful centerpiece in this New York loft space. The delivery address and the "handle with care" label are still attached from the time the crate was delivered, which only add to its charm.

Above right A well-traveled leather trunk with signs of wear has taken on a less demanding role as a coffee table. It is also very useful as storage for magazines and newspapers, and is the perfect height to serve as a footstool.

Two different takes on a coffee table, but both great examples of upcycling

The ingenious coffee table shown on the left came about purely by accident. It is made up of a packing crate of pressed chipboard, which originally held some kitchen doors delivered when the family was renovating their home. As they had no furniture at the time, they used the crate as a makeshift coffee table, but then grew to love it, especially as their name and address are written on the side, together with a "handle with care" label, making it a truly personal piece of furniture. The simplicity of design and the modest materials complement this loft space particularly well and also suit the enormous, comfortable seating modules.

In the picture above, the slouchy, natural linen sofas are complemented by a rather battered old leather trunk that has been upcycled as a coffee table. It also provides storage and acts as a giant footstool. It is both sturdy and functional, and because leather looks great mixed with natural linen, trunks and suitcases in all materials make great side tables and coffee tables. They require no adjustment and no remodeling.

Rescued from a French barn undergoing renovation, this exterior door now has a brand new purpose in life. Its faded, weatherbeaten colors perfectly complement the pale flagstone floor.

The term "upcycled" often suggests something utilitarian and practical, but here are two examples of what can be achieved with a little imagination. All it takes is to look at something with a fresh eye—forget its original use and explore its new possibilities.

This wooden French door is a great example of how something old can be adapted for another everyday purpose. Supported by cinder blocks set at an angle, it makes a perfect coffee table, its rusted hinges and metal studs adding to its intrinsic beauty.

Left This attractive wood and metal trunk is now employed to provide useful storage, but it comes with a sense of history and adventure. It looks both masculine and sophisticated in a living-room setting.

creative displays

These three interiors have a number of things in common but the most interesting is the oversized scale of the furniture compared to the size of the rooms. Making the rooms comfortable was the reason behind the design decisions made, as well as a desire to incorporate the large pieces of art in the space. Big soft sofas, cushions, and throws deliver the required degree of comfort, while their textures and tones complement the paintings on the walls.

On paper, the different elements in these rooms might seem totally at odds but in reality they work incredibly well together. For example, in the picture on the right, the imposing Viramontes painting makes an unexpected but totally effective backdrop to the plaster statue of Leda and the Swan, a motif from Greek mythology, displayed appropriately on the capital of a classical-style column. Also unlikely in terms of pairing is the floor-standing iron candlestick from Mexico but its inclusion is inspired. Such eclectic elements give a home its individuality.

Above A sense of drama is created with this idiosyncratic combination of a romantic painting by the French artist Laurence Amélie, an oversized sofa, a statue of the Madonna, and a chunky wooden crucifix.

Left With the ocean the backdrop to this Malibu house and also to the painting, this work by the Italian artist Ubaldo Franceschini has found the perfect home.

Opposite An imposing piece of art by Tony Viramontes, the American fashion illustrator, makes a bold statement that complements the dramatic quality of the interior.

Have the courage of your convictions to make unlikely alliances in your displays

What I find most striking about the decoration of this living space is the collection of Indian art and mirrors gathered together on one wall. It works so well because their shapes and finish are all complementary. Enforcing the ethnic feel, as well as adding color and texture, are the kilim pillows and a throw from Uzbekistan.

Left and above The beautifully worn glass mercury mirror in the living room reflects the time-worn nature of the space. Either side is an early portrait and a vintage seascape hanging in the old-fashioned way from metal picture hangers. Three sofas, one deep-buttoned with mismatching pillows, the other two in raw natural linen and decorated with stitched Indian throws, give off a bohemian air. The unusual occasional table has turned cotton reel legs. On top sits a wooden hat mold purely for decoration.

There may be a casual feel to this light-filled living space, but it has in fact been furnished and decorated in a carefully curated way. The Manhattan apartment takes up the whole of the first floor of an 1850s building that was previously a garment factory. The owner rents the dilapidated apartment from a sculptor who had lived there since the 1960s. He has restored it to make it comfortable for everyday living, while retaining all the original features and, in most cases, the original patina.

Old and retired objects feature throughout and add to the sense of history that already exists. Vintage textiles and kilims are thrown over sofas to soften their hard edges, and wonderful collectibles are displayed on walls and tables, creating exquisite still-life moments.

Another view of the living room on the previous page. Reflected in the pockmarked mirror are an old artist's testing board and one of the many table lamps that contribute to the relaxing feel. Pillows made from an eclectic mix of fabrics, including an old kilim and ticking, are scattered casually on the sofas. The glass of water on the tray is for Skip, the owner's elderly cat, to drink from.

modern retro

The prevailing look in this amazing west London home is modernist, but the owners have cleverly woven in other elements, mixing different styles, to create a stunning yet unpretentious space where everyone feels immediately welcome. It is furnished with wide, 1960s-style armchairs and cushions in retro-style fabrics. These, together with the floor lamp, with its black pleated shade and legs like a tripod, and the glass-topped side table, create a comfortable nook for reading and watching TV.

The neutral-colored walls provide the ideal backdrop for an esoteric collection of art. A keen eye for contemporary British art is evident in the oil on canvas by Philip Davies.

Left The newly upholstered 1950s chairs are unfussy additions to the corner of this living room. The diminutive granddaughter clock was given to the owner's grandparents in the 1930s as a wedding present and has enormous sentimental value.

Above Splashes of yellow from the silk cushion and original occasional table—an unbelievable find at a flea market—and the blue of the 1950s armchair are eye-catching color combinations. The words on the John Derian decoupage plate sum up the decor of this home very simply: "Things I like"!

Right The bright living room, with all the original cornicing, is painted in a pale, neutral shade that tones down the effect of the white wooden shutters. Hanging from the ceiling is a slatted cedarwood lamp from the Finnish company Secto Design. Two gray-fabric, mid-20th-century-style sofas and a sage-green, silk-mix rug are simple but comfortable additions.

This Manhattan apartment is utterly compelling. The long sash windows bring natural light into the open-plan living area. The walls have been taken back to the raw brick and painted white, a striking contrast against the dark wood polished floorboards, lightening the space even further. The dark colors of the furniture—the mid-20th-century leather sofa, the glossy black coffee table, and the early 1960s Harvey Probber velvet club chair—are also offset to perfection by the white walls.

The George Nelson floor lamp emits a golden glow to the space. Just one piece of wall art— a Martyn Thompson photograph—is all that's needed to decorate this side of the apartment.

The living room from the previous page is viewed here from the kitchen. A net of pea lights has been strung across the three windows, giving the space a magical quality, as well as providing some privacy. The wooden struts to the sides are supports for the bedrooms above.

This room, known to the homeowners as the den, is where everyone relaxes and watches TV. It's a comfortable mix of retro and modern, and has clearly been decorated and furnished with meticulous care and a distinctive style. The dark, painted walls are in contrast to the white in the rest of the house (glimpsed seen through the open door above), giving the den a cozy feel. A color palette of predominantly brown and cream for the furniture enhances the effect.

Above left The brown sofa, with cushions covered in a 1950s green splash fabric, add a subtle hint of color amid the overall dark tones. Spotlighting the rich brown walls is a modern, black, angled floor lamp. The antler lamp was made by their friend Liddy Holt.

Above An abstract painting by Andrew Egan hangs above the Danish Modern folding chair by Ebert Wells.

On the television screen, you can see a reflection of the wall seen on pages 50–51: there is a complete contrast between that and this uncompromising black wall. The mid-century modern silver sofa and armchair only add to the drama of the room.

This cozy nook is in fact a screening room, where the owners can relax and read from the shelves of art books, or watch a movie or the television. Original G Plan armchairs, reupholstered by Pitfield London, are perfectly placed for relaxation either side of a vintage French lamp on top of a mid-20th-century, glass-topped coffee table. The shelves are also home to a collection of ceramics, including large-scale retro pieces from Germany and the more delicate and finer English china of Hornsea and Denby. The original artwork on the left-hand wall is from a Christmas card made by the owner's textiles tutor, Natalie Gibson.

In this library, specially designed fitted shelves are full to the brim with books, all of them logged by theme, covering subjects from Japanese architecture to plants and flowers, and everything in between. The 1960s sofa and two chairs, with their fake bamboo frames, are decorated with a selection of Fornasetti printed cushions. A porcelain cat has made itself at home on the "bamboo" coffee table.

CHAPTER 3

WORK & CREATE

HOME OFFICES

Left This designer has filled her work space with objects that are the source of her inspiration. Fabric swatches are stored in woven boxes, ready to be delved into whenever needed. The pinboard is home to an array of photos and other personal mementos.

Above More well covered pinboards, but this time with magazine clippings that are useful for this designer's work, as well as a reminder of what she has achieved.

Working from home can be lonely at times, so a work space that is comfortable and personal is as important as having all the right components to do the task at hand. Only then is the mind truly free to wander and think blissfully of the next big thing.

The office seen here represents the creative hub in separate locations of a truly inspiring designer. Both are private spaces where she can immerse herself in the pictures, photos, and colors of her world. A sketch found in a flea market could inspire a piece of furniture, while a snip of fabric could be reproduced to create a new line of bed linen. Although small, these details speak volumes to her. Pinned to a board, they are reminders and ideas that can be used in her designs at a later date, while pictures of loved ones simply make her smile.

Exquisitely chosen art and pictures give this home office in a light-filled New York apartment a cool authority. The owners know exactly what they like and live a life surrounded by those elements. Everything is very considered and sophisticated, without being contrived, and the overall feel is one of comfort.

Although the decoration is predominantly monochrome, it is not at all hard-edged. A number of objects with personal appeal—such as the canvas destination board or the soft toy on the desk—are dotted among fine designer pieces. Not only does this room say a lot about its owners, in particular their impeccable eye for design and detail, but it also offers an insight into what makes them tick.

Above A beautiful glass lamp sits on a neat, well-organized office table. The uniform yellow pencils, probably used more as decoration than for writing, further illustrate the organized nature of the room and introduce a splash of color.

Right The most striking feature in this home office is a floor-to-ceiling canvas destination board from a Melbourne tram, evoking memories of time spent in that city.

The focus of this home office in a converted barn is the memory board of concert tickets, made out of four industrial metal frames. The wood-paneled wall is in stark contrast to the thick stone walls elsewhere in this French home, and is evidence of how the owners enjoy living among contrasting styles. Many design features have been added to the barn, including the recess in the room beyond, which houses a statue of the Hindu god Ganesha, brought back from a trip to India.

Filling this first-floor office space is an eclectic mixture of items. A print of a phrenology head is propped up against an enormous abstract mural by the French artist Aurelie Alvarez. The canvas bag in front of the antique desk is by Leslie Oschmann from her Swarm collection.

CREATIVE STUDIOS

Surrounded by windows, which allow the space to be filed with light, this is the studio of a renowned candle designer— a room in a little wooden house that she calls her witch's cottage. It was built in the 1900s and its setting is idyllic, nestled at the base of the Hollywood Hills, right below the famous "Hollywood" sign, and with breathtaking views of the canyon below. The wooden, folding art table, which once belonged to her artist father, forms the heart of her working life. Decades olds, it is a beautiful piece of furniture in its own right.

Left The creative world of this designer revolves around her desk. This very precious piece of furniture belonged to her father, an artist, and in itself never fails to inspire her. The large, majestic candle holder to the left of the picture is a vintage find from Mexico and the perfect platform for displaying one of her creations.

Right An ordered display of treasured and beautiful images—picture postcards, magazine cuttings, even notes from friends—pinned to the wall is an enduring piece of inspiration. The antique brass lamp, with its seductive curves, is practical as well as good-looking.

Full of character, this work space is the creative center for a talented young designer

artistic spaces

Sometimes, just because of the nature of your work, beauty is created by accident, and it is the unexpected and the imperfect that are so appealing. The studio seen on the right belongs to an artist who embraces the art created by the paint splashes she makes as she works. Her pots start life as purely practical containers for her brushes but then take on an artistic role themselves, covered in the trademark colors that she uses for her painting.

The location of the work space on the left, a château in Paris, couldn't be grander, but the desk is simplicity itself. As the owner sets to work, all her practical needs are met by her notebooks and something to write with. But what makes the space so appealing is the vase of green hydrangeas and the lustrous coffee cup and milk pitcher in an equally vivid turquoise.

Left The beauty of imperfection is clear to see in this Parisian château. Peeling wallpaper and the worn and dilapidated woodwork create a rare beauty and are a gracious backdrop to a simple working space.

Right The artist who owns this studio has a delicate hand with color, fusing it with nature, as shown in these paintings of flowers.

Tucked away in a side street in Hove, on England's south coast, this artist's studio is in a run-down yet picturesque stable, part of an 18th-century mews. A small and intimate space, it is completely lined in panels of wood and painted white. The practical reason for the soft wood walls is that they can be drilled with screws, wherever necessary or convenient, to allow the hanging of pictures and the pinning of sketches.

As for many artists, postcard collections are an inspiration as well as a convenient aide-mémoire for recalling color combinations, an approach to a piece of work, or even just an attitude.

These three wall panels show different parts of the same studio. The postcards, pinned to the soft wood walls, provide inspiration for the artist. Hanging to the right of them is a group of the artist's own tests for color or texture. A dried seed pod and a piece of driftwood give a sense of what the artist wants to paint, while the swatch card is an illustration of what can be achieved.

Under the clock, the small picture of an artist at work is a gentle reminder of all those artists over the centuries who have toiled in difficult and uncomfortable environments.

Working in earth colors, the artist has smeared and noted many shades of brown and carefully mixed each with a little white to show how they all react to a lightening agent. Some colors become much greener, some more golden; some are very intense pigments, while others are delicately transparent.

While no longer used by the owner for his daily work, this first-floor studio still has echoes of that time. The design tools still hang in the same place they always used to, above the "Riga e Squadra" desk that he designed himself. Everything is well ordered and tidy, precious and cared for. The space is filled with pieces of personal value that are clear expressions of the owner's playful sense of humor.

Left There is so much to look at in this photograph. The plaster hand holding a pencil draws the eye first, and this is to me almost a statement of what the room was used for. It is based on the hand of David in the statue by Michelangelo. A religious icon by the staircase sits next to a vintage Fornasetti butterfly obelisk lamp. Beneath, a pair of ceramic soldiers' boots is used to hold long paintbrushes. Keeping an eye on you as you climb the stairs to the study above is a quirky metal cat, a gift from the cat's creator, artist Fabius Tita.

Provocative words as well as images inform this artist's playful approach to her work

Although small, the work space of this artist contains everything she needs for both the practical and the creative aspects of her work in visual imagery and origami. To one side is a tall and functional shelf unit containing work files and many reference books, topped with pots of paintbrushes and other equipment. Her approach to her work is playful, sometimes irreverent, which is reflected in her choice of found print covering the wall in front of the desk. Cut-outs and quotes, some of a provocative nature, are all ideas and inspirations for her ever-changing and thoughtful designs. They fuel her desire to experiment with printed matter and discover new ways in which to make collages and geometric shapes in art.

Left A comfortable chair and an ordered desk, combined with an idiosyncratic wall display, are characteristic of a hard-working artist, who works in an environment that suits her creativity perfectly.

Right A page of a sketch book lies open on the desk. The book contains a mix of drawings of people in the public eye and those not famous at all, pointing to the artist's need to draw reference from the world around her. Two examples of her paper art sit side by side, each testament to her incredible skill.

Left When seated at her desk, this artist has everything to hand to enable her to design her beautiful pieces of origami.

This artist's beautiful paintings have a clear and defined style, which is then reflected in her work space—well ordered and neat.

The very ordered studio of an
artist/designer who is methodical
and whose work requires very
few tools, hence the neatness
of the space.

Above The briefcase on this desk, and its contents, symbolize a make-believe business. A complete installation, this was created by the designer for a recent exhibition.

Right Two computer-generated images representative of this artist's work, a red pot containing pencils and pens, and a few rough sketches all show signs of work in progress.

Simplicity is key to this studio space. A plain wooden desk and a white plastic chair are the only pieces of furniture needed by this artist-designer, while a pristine white PC and keyboard are the only real tools necessary for him to navigate his artistic adventure. His art is striking and tends to be on the dark side, but the colorful computer-generated images on the wall and desk give the space a playful, pop-art feel. A clamp-on metal desk lamp, a few pens, and a cutting board hint at the intricate processes that take place during the development of his work.

Unused.
not
Wanted.
Take me

These individual pieces of framed art have all been created by the owner. The bright and dark colors, and the different textures, forms, and media coexist well in this living/working space.

SERVICIO
DOMICILIO

7

FLAVIO CONCEIÇÃO

Fresas

TCÉTERA
Y TAL

The living/working environment created by this illustrator proudly boasts an abundance of art—a wacky collection of forms and colors. There is a humorous aspect to most of the pieces, with references and influences from a number of different sources. Using many textures and forms, the owner works hard, constantly visualizing the next big thing, the next idea, or simply the next artwork. To be in this environment provides him with a constant source of inspiration.

A bright yellow coat, together with the straw fedoras sat on a chair, are personal reminders of the owner who lives as well as works with this collection of unique and individual art.

fashion designers

This young fashion designer's home is also her work space, in this divine house near Venice Beach. To get to work, she just has to walk from her bedroom into this creative space, where she immerses herself immediately in her craft. The light and airy room speaks volumes about her world of fashion and is filled with all the elements that she finds inspiring. She can spend hours drawing and thinking of her next creations at the large and weathered table.

Left By the wall, and reflected in the beautiful carved vintage mirror, is an old tailor's dummy, ready for pinning with new designs, which helps to establish a sense of color and proportion. Rails of vintage clothes are reflected in the modern, floor-to-ceiling mirror. These elements are not only practical and inspirational but also decoration for the space.

Above and right At the top of the house, overlooking the street below, is this well-organized and tidy work space of a clothes designer and photographer. A selection of favorite found objects, all of them inspirational in their own way, line the windowsill, while a piece of vintage linen lies on the desk. Photographs of loved ones are an appropriate addition to this deeply personal work space.

Next page A sun-filled, third-floor room is the home studio of a dress designer who is in the throes of designing gowns for flamboyant entertainers. The practical tasks of cutting and sewing take place here but so, too, does the initial creativity. He has a very clear vision of the direction in which he wants to take his designs, and he surrounds himself with those things from which he can draw inspiration. The looming print of Damien Hirst's jeweled skull "For the Love of God" and several other skull references are among them.

inspire ... and smile ...

The vivid and magpie imagination of this clothes designer is apparent everywhere you look in his studio, which is seen from a different angle on the previous page. A large, upside-down triangle hanging on the wall is used for storing the colorful threads that he uses every day, while on the shelf above stands the white figurine of a cartoon character. An ornate heart-shaped mirror adds a touch of vintage glamour to the space.

CHAPTER 4

SLEEP & BATHE

CREATIVE BEDROOMS

Where we sleep should be a sanctuary—our safe haven from the world, and a place of rest. Decoration in this room of the house is often more minimal, but certain touches can stop it from feeling impersonal or cold.

The plain white bed linen in this sunny bedroom helps to create a calm and relaxing environment. The gray-on-white abstract painting and the curved night table soften what could otherwise be a rather stark room.

A small black vintage lamp sits on the curved white chest, alongside a tree ornament with delicate flowers found in a Long Island antique store. Sprayed with white paint, it adds to the cohesion of the room. Magazines are kept close at hand, but neatly stored away in a rack beside the bed.

The large master bedroom in this bright apartment is tranquil and refined, with a crisp, clean, and well-thought-out appearance. Decorative details are kept to a minimum, but those present add the character to the room. Above the bed are a set of three rare Victorian prints of men in period costume, underlined by the white linen headboard. Either side, and in contrast, hang two 1930s fashion plates of men in rather formal suiting.

Dark brown, ribbed pottery lamps with stark white linen shades sit on each side of the bed and tie in with the dark frames of the photos, creating a cohesive look. Softening the overall effect is a beautiful white embroidered bed throw, twinkling with tiny mirrors. The enormous mirror on the wall opposite the bed reflects much of the scene, while the pictures reflect the shutters at the south-facing window.

Above Rare Victorian and 1930s prints in plain black frames, reflected in the enormous mirror, are the focus of this simple but sophisticated bedroom. The frames detract nothing from the pictures themselves, while reflections of the shutters on the glass are a subtle embellishment. The vertical radiator blends almost seamlessly into the white wall.

Plain black frames protect the rare prints and don't get in the way of them telling their stories

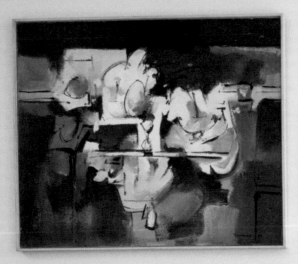

Soothing, comfortable, and almost monochrome, this master bedroom features floor-to-ceiling doors opening out onto the garden that fill the room with light. A 1950s French articulated lamp sits by the bed on the white Saarinen table. The metal-framed glass table on wheels is a 1955 Bauhaus design, its clean lines kept free of extraneous clutter. The gorgeous cushion covers are made from 1960s headscarves.

A subtle mural gives this bedroom with
its awkward ceiling a unique fluid feel.
The palette of warm colors and stream
of broken light make the wall calm and
easy on the eye.

Although vintage, the gasoline sign over the bed gives this bedroom a thoroughly modern and industrial feel. A masculine vibe is softened by the use of mainly neutral colors, as well as by the pillows heaped upon the bed.

When buying items for your home, you need to visualize what they will look like in the intended location. The young DJ who lives here is a collector of all things unusual with a real magpie instinct. He came across old metal signs and various discarded items and could picture them in his home. It took an inspired eye to see that the gasoline sign would look superb on the wall above the bed, and that the "Pupo" marble slab, picked up from the roadside, could also become a wall decoration.

Below The poisons cabinet is a bold choice but provides the perfect place to store shoes. The chunk of marble hanging above the cabinet, with a child's gas mask on top, tells us that the owner is not afraid to take a few decorating risks. The goldfish in a glass bowl represents a certain hominess in this quirky space.

Left Battered old suitcases offer a unique bedside table and complement the vintage shutters. The miniature chair ornament on top of the suitcases adds a modern retro touch.

Folding wooden shutters block out the sun and noise from the street below in this Manhattan apartment. The original, raw wooden floorboards and soft, creamy walls give the space an overall softness and unique charm. The old wooden table by the bed is home to another collection of precious found objects. A small, delicate crystal chandelier hangs from the ceiling.

More views of the bedroom from the previous page. The chunky form of the original, low-level radiator contrasts with the very delicate vintage chair alongside. The chair has been newly upholstered in cream linen, while the cover tucked into the end of the spindly metal-framed bed is made of white cotton.

Right An upturned, zinc water tank has a new lease of life as the most imaginative and effective bedside table. On top, a wooden mushroom lends a raw, decorative touch, while the twisted and gilded wooden lamp base adds glamour.

Peeling paint, cracked plaster, and well-worn floorboards evoke times long past

Wood-lined walls create an earthy and calm feel in this relaxation space. They are bespoke and made from untreated wood. The owner hand-picked every single piece of wood for the wall to give it the desired random and color-mismatch look.

The double doors are bespoke, too. They are simple in design, and basic gilt catches are used as fastenings. An unusual feature, they perfectly complement the walls.

Little other decoration is needed here. Covering the bed is a ceremonial marriage blanket from Morocco, which adds warmth—stylistically, as well as literally—to the room.

Left The landing, which leads to the bedrooms and bathroom, is very simply decorated, with a black-painted handrail and bare, industrial-style light bulb.

Right The bed is covered with a gorgeous, glittery Moroccan wedding blanket, a glamorous counterpoint to the slatted wood wall.

A wall of sheer voile curtains hides windows and highlights this bed and the selection of cushions in Florence Broadhurst prints. A piece of ethereal art of Coney Island by Lisa Andrew forms the backdrop to an enormous fern and a weathered and beaten-up old chair. Much too dilapidated to sit on, the chair adds character to the room.

Different styles rub shoulders easily with one another in this master bedroom. The paneled walls and doors have been lovingly restored to their Georgian splendor, but the decoration is much more contemporary. A piece of 1960s metal wall art by Curtis Jeré hangs over the deep-buttoned, duck-egg-blue headboard. Similarly tactile is the heavily embroidered Chinese silk bedcover. Combined, these elements create a very calm and restful space.

Always rem
Forgive quic
Laugh in lo
And never
Made you o

using display

It's always tempting to go for the safe option when decorating our bedrooms, even though it's so easy to create fascinating displays with the simplest of objects, provided you put them together in a clever way. The owner's confident style shines through in this beautiful but simple bedroom, with a well-chosen verse in elegant script on the wall alongside a pair of naturally shed antlers, a vintage gown, and pure linen sheets.

Everything about this bedroom is elegant and calm, created primarily by the cream color scheme. A simple black stool acts as a night table for an equally simple lamp.

Two bedrooms within a rural retreat in upstate New York are featured here. Each is simply decorated with great impact. The main bedroom, above, sets a spectacular mosaic washstand against a white wall and plain linen, allowing it to be the focus of the room. Although the washstand is a modern Ercole piece, it has a strongly vintage feel, and will become an heirloom for the future. A small framed picture has been hung above the washstand and complements it perfectly.

In the guest bedroom, pretty tiled tables, along with vintage candleholder bedside lights, add just the right amount of interest to the room. As a room used less often, the guest bedroom is the ideal place to display treasured ornaments such as vintage ceramics.

Above The cabinet next to the bed is an Ercole mosaic washstand. Broken pieces of vintage china, in a curlicue pattern dotted with butterflies, make up its top. The cupboard doors are painted green, and vintage wallpaper has been laid in the door panels. The delicate metal framework of the bed and the vintage candleholder are romantic extras.

Left Decorative vintage candleholders make gorgeous bedside lights. This ornate example, made from Italian glass, is set off to perfection against the sheer, white cotton shade.

Below left A small square table with a tiled top holds yet another decorative lamp. The quality bed linen, in soft tones with an embroidered trim, is perfect for a guest room.

Below The vintage oil painting on canvas in this guest bedroom depicts fairies in a garden. Its whimsical subject matter strikes a chord with the small decorative console shelf beneath and the vintage ceramic deer and cart.

Black-and-white photographs
of revered icons and family and
friends make a strong theme for
hanging art in this bright bedroom

Black-and-white photography as a theme for wall art is deservedly popular because it is easy to create something quite striking with it. The subject matter of this collection of black-and-white photos and paintings ranges from the owners' favorite icons taken by famous photographers to well-loved images of friends and family. The balance, form, and shapes that you create on the wall with your photographs are crucial to its success. Big pictures are best hung centrally. Although the display here appears ordered and straight, there is a slight random quality to it, which increases the appeal.

The bedroom is suffused with natural light, as you can see from the reflections of the shutters. Illuminating the wall, this natural light sets off the art to perfection.

Above This guest bedroom, with white walls and simple white bedside tables provides the perfect blank canvas or hanging favorite black-and-white images of icons and family and friends. The frames, which are of various sizes, are grouped strategically together on one wall for maximum effect. Natural light pours into the room from the window opposite, filtered through the shutters. Reflections in the glass heighten the display. The lone cherub above the bed adds a humorous touch.

Above A wooden and metal cart acts as functional storage for towels and toiletries. Above the bed hangs a Le Klint pendant light.

bedside furniture

This simply designed bedroom is found inside a quirky Victorian house, where the owners have mixed various periods and materials with great success. Wood and metal combine to create an industrial feel, while the pendant light softens the look with its modern retro curves. Repurposing items, such as the filing cabinets and stool, gives a sense of age while still achieving a certain freshness. Each piece of furniture is different from the others, but the dark brown walls and clever use of accessories brings everything together.

A simple but bold decorating style gives a real urban quality to this period house

Above left Vintage brushed-steel filing cabinets are used to hold the small television and telephone.

Left An original 1930s Anglepoise lamp, restored to working order, sits on top of the tall cabinet made from different pieces of recycled wood. White shades filter the light through this dark but well-put-together room.

Above A stool, possibly once used in a light industrial space during the 1930s, has been cleverly converted into a bedside table. The lamp on top, restored and recycled from original pieces, adds a solitary splash of color.

Left The bedroom in this beautiful modern home has a single wall decorated with wallpaper. Resembling a line drawing, the monochrome pattern of looming trees is very striking and adds a unique dimension to the room. The wooden bird on the bedside shelf completes the forest theme.

Right In the foreground, sat on a small white table, is a large Diptyque candle. The small Saarinen table displays carefully selected items, in shades of gray, black, and silver. The tall black floor lamp is by Flos.

Above Illuminating a display of French neoclassical prints is a bizarre bedside lamp with a stem of ostrich eggshells and a shade of guinea fowl feathers. The small glass-topped table also holds framed family pictures and a plant, which contribute to this carefully constructed decorative scheme.

Left The reflection of this amazing bedroom in the ornate oval mirror is a display in its own right. The brave choice of yellow toile de Jouy for the bed makes a dramatic impact against the pale stone of the walls.

Left A delightful French antique dressing table is trimmed with green. The color has formed the basis of the room's decoration: a green tin, a green vase, and a bold embroidery with green highlights hanging above the bed unite the display.

Below On a vintage nightstand, a pink glass lamp with a lace shade creates an utterly feminine and romantic aesthetic in this Malibu beach house. Reflected in the mirror is an enchanting oil painting of a young girl, perfectly positioned on the opposite wall.

Small pieces of decorative furniture play a big role in enhancing a room

Left A mix of religious and cultural references and materials comes together to make a perfectly balanced display. Hanging from the dark gray-painted wall, the copy of a 1970s plaster panel taken from the ceiling of London's Southwark Cathedral makes a suitably solid backdrop to the large Chinese bamboo and cane chest with the display of leather boxes and a stone Buddha on top.

Right In this bedroom, behind the large, ribbed, onion-shaped vase on the nightstand, designed by Michael Reeves, stands a gesso screen, with a wall lamp in gold leaf on metal. These elements are at perfect ease with the unusually shaped white linen headboard, resulting in a haven of well-designed masculinity.

Below A custom-made commode, with an elegant, shiny lamp on top, doubles up as a bedside table. These two elements make the room feel both glamorous and highly chic.

These three well-presented spaces (the rooms above, left, and opposite are in the same home) have each been designed with every consideration for their owners' needs and to reflect their personalities. They share the same design approach—chic and minimalist with a masculine aesthetic—and the highest quality materials have been used throughout. These elements, combined with a restrained, often monochromatic, color palette, have produced exclusive, well-considered spaces, with an enviable and very well-designed decoration.

Right, opposite, and below The neutral complementary colors chosen for this master bedroom merge together seamlessly, creating a warm and cozy display. The distressed antique furniture keeps the atmosphere informal.

In this master bedroom, soft harmonious colors—cream, pale gray, blush pink—are well balanced with texture and the imperfection of antiques. A pair of vintage octagonal mirrors either side of the bed is a bold but successful addition. All the choices made here, from the soft mohair throw and cushions on the chairs, to the velvet quilted throw draped over the end of the bed and the deep-buttoned, linen-covered bed head, are carefully considered, and together they create a restful and luxurious retreat. This airy, sunny bedroom is a true haven of relaxation.

BATHROOMS

The bathroom is a purely functional room, but one that need not lose out on design: ideally, the same calming atmosphere of the bedroom should extend into this essential space.

This modern bathroom has an immediate sense of tranquility. Huge windows with white curtains allow light to fill the room. Muted gray, skimmed concrete walls form the backdrop to a long, white trough basin. The built-in storage underneath the sink means clutter is kept to a minimum. The chrome fittings are modern and streamlined, adding to the quietly efficient ambience.

In this streamlined and pared-back haven of peace and quiet, gray, skimmed concrete walls form a soothing backdrop for the contemporary chrome fittings and white, ceramic trough sink.

Despite the beautiful traditional roll-top bathtub, the bathroom above has a contemporary feel. The white and silver color scheme creates a clean and soothing atmosphere, which is only enhanced by the view of the garden below.

The bathroom on the right is a completely modern, sleek space, with state-of-the-art enamel fixtures and chrome fittings. It is, however, not without character, thanks to the inclusion of decorative elements such as the colored glass bottles and the silver sputnik light.

Above Although contemporary, the clear acrylic Philippe Starck Ghost chairs either side of the tub have a sophistication that complements the traditional roll-top bathtub. Silver fabric cushions on top add a touch of glamour. A small chrome decorative table holds a posy of white roses and a scented candle ready to burn.

Above A carefully arranged display of colored retro glass bottles is a fitting decorative addition to this bathroom, contrasting beautifully with the sleek chrome taps and streamlined enamel bathtub.

Right The molded plastic caddy with swing-out trays for holding bathroom toiletries is a design classic on casters by Joe Colombo from the 1970s, originally used by architects as an office organizer. Above, the 1960s Chrome Pistillo sputnik light fitting sends out shafts of light. Large rectangular white tiles cover the walls, floor, and bath surround, giving a unified look.

This guest bedroom in the same house as the bathroom on the previous page again makes use of colored retro glass bottles on a simple glass shelf to create an attractive display. A soya candle with a cotton wick by Cire Trudon, portraying a classical bust, makes a lovely decorative bookend to the glass collection. In spite of its sound ecological credentials, the candle will probably never be burned, simply because it would ruin the display. A light well clad in dark wood directs additional light onto the shelf.

On the right is a bathroom that is more art deco in style. A bold geometric pattern of yellow and white tiles on the walls and floor and complementary fittings are accompanied by metal wall art from the 1960s and a vintage gilt chandelier. The different styles and periods rub shoulders easily with one another, proving that you need not stick slavishly to one theme only.

Left Daylight streams down through the light well, illuminating the display of glass bottles and the candle in the shape of a classical bust.

Simple decorative displays of retro glass bottles in different colors give personality to otherwise purely functional spaces

Mixing styles and periods is the best way to be the most expressive in your home

Above These yellow and white tiles are by Moderna, laid in a striking geometric pattern. Metallic wall art by Curtis Jeré adorns the walls, while a vintage gilt chandelier is the perfect partner to the art.

Left A huge and heavy dark wood mirror adds contrast to the tiles but does not look out of place in the slightest.

The sparkling whites of the brick wall tiles and the roll-top bath, combined with natural materials and grouped collectibles, give this bathroom the feel of an idyllic retreat.

Seashells are often considered the perfect accessory for the bathroom, but used unimaginatively they can be a decorative cliché. That, most definitely, is not the case here. The exquisite fan of coral protected under glass and a collage of shells, starfish, and sand set behind a battered antique frame are glorious artworks. On either side are antique train luggage racks, an inspired choice for storing towels.

The vintage bathroom stand is a real find. A tall chrome shaving mirror runs through the center of the wooden table. Attached to it are brushed-steel bowls for shaving foam and water. Candles fixed to the mirror hint at the age of the piece.

Right A tranquil bathroom space with distinctive artwork displaying sea treasures, such as coral, tiny pebbles, and starfish. Antique train luggage racks are an inventive but practical solution for storing fine cotton towels and hanging shiny mother-of-pearl shells.

These pictures are of two different bathrooms in the same home, which is a treasure-trove of unexpected delights. The owners are avid collectors on a constant quest to find new and interesting items but they do so with a disciplined eye. They are able to put together powerful themes without falling victim to random finds that have no real focus and would weaken a display.

The guest bathroom on the left has a strong naval and coastal theme. Filling an entire wall, striking images of ocean liners, navy boats, proud naval officers in uniform, and a beautiful, embroidered naval emblem are the apt and attractive subject matter of this very small space.

The image to the right offers a different view of the bathroom shown on the previous page. Here, too, the wall art revolves around water, with a restrained theme of seashore-collected items. The shiny porcelain tiles and the natural cotton towels are set off by strings of mother-of-pearl shells, coral, and natural sponges.

Above All these naval theme pictures were discovered at antique markets and fairs. Although they are of various shapes and sizes, and never previously formed part of a collection, their shared subject matter gives them a unity. Ships, portraits of officers, and emblems, all hanging in attractive frames, share the wall space in a most orderly fashion.

Right The seaside theme in this bathroom is as far from a cliché as you can imagine. The old train luggage rack provides storage for the towels, which hang alongside strings of shiny shells.

In the guest bedroom, a Victorian floral hand basin, on an aged metal stand, is surrounded by exposed copper pipes, some of them covered in verdigris. A white table acts as a dressing table with the carved Ethiopian chair. Giving a blast of color and modernity is the quirky piece of art by Henry Villiers.

Right As well as a circular brass shower curtain rail and a basin in the corner, this bathroom is home to a black-painted roll-top bathtub, which suits the age of the house perfectly, matching the Victorian bathroom fixtures.

There is no shortage of wood in these two rooms, which are both in the same period property. The main bathroom includes bespoke floor-to-ceiling cupboards—a great form of storage—as well as dark brown floorboards, while wood paneling in the guest room has been painted white.

All the bathroom fixtures are Victorian, but with up-to-date plumbing. In the guest room, the owner has plumbed in 19th-century faucets and used exposed copper pipes to give the space an air of authenticity.

CHILDREN'S ROOMS

What should I do with my child's bedroom?" is a question often asked by parents but actually the answer couldn't be easier, simply because children constantly create their own decorative material that can be used and updated as they get older and become more sophisticated. Their original drawings and paintings, photographs of sporting and academic achievements and parties—the list is endless—can all be displayed.

In this seven-year-old's bedroom, an entire wall is covered in framed photographs of family friends, self-portraits, parties, and gifts from grandparents and godparents. The display is not only deeply personal but also very attractive and creative.

When embarking on the adventure of creating wall art for a child's bedroom, first gather together with them all the photos they love the best. Then move on to certificates of achievement, the favorite artworks they've created, and precious toys or special possessions that may need the protection of a shadow box. Dig around in closets and pull out those dearly loved (and suitable) items that deserve to be seen but up until now haven't had a home.

For the wall art in a child's room to really work, it needs to be collaborative. Put aside some time when you can sit down with them and encourage them to choose their favorite things, while steering them discreetly in a direction that you would like them to go. Young children, in particular, will probably soon tire of the task but they will come back to it. Photographs of parents and grandparents, family pets, friends, and favorite teachers can all be considered, while special events, such as school plays and fancy-dress parties, can provide the most entertaining images.

Once your child has made their choice, start collecting suitable frames. These don't have to be expensive, nor any particular color—mixing and matching can be very effective. Above all, the wall art needs to be fun, eye-catching, and representative of the spirit of your child. It is something they will be proud of and will want to share with others. Add a chalkboard to the mix for conveying messages, reminders, and thoughts for the day.

Above and right These close-ups are of the wall shown on the previous page. Photographs of family and memorable occasions have been given a funky look using a graphics editing program. Cherished toys are displayed in box frames, while christening gifts have been mounted and framed.

Getting a teenager to share your vision and aesthetic of what their bedroom should look like is rarely easy. It's important for them to be able to express themselves in their own way but this needn't mean that the look is offensive to you. In this bedroom, a beautiful space has been created, which gently reflects the style of the rest of the home without compromising on the teenager's individuality and sense of style. A slightly haphazard selection of different-size gold letters spells out in no uncertain terms this teenager's name, triumphantly heralding that the space belongs to her. The vintage crystal chandelier adds a dash of charm and glamour.

Created with her mother's help, this special space, where the teenager can enjoy her privacy in carefully chosen surroundings, is the envy of all her friends. The room is designed in such a way that it is easy to keep tidy, which was an important factor for the mother. The space is simple, with plenty of room to spread out and study, and even to try on clothes. Natural and pure accessories are an important feature of the home, and also of this room—the bed, for example, is covered with pure linen sheets. Such elements help to give this room an identity and an aesthetic that complement the rest of the home.

Left Painted black, the door to the room acts as a chalkboard— dramatic and personal, as well as practical.

Right Gold letters in different sizes spell out this teenager's name and proudly stamp her identity on the space.

MIZZY

Grouping
similar collected
images together
can create
a unified and
colorful piece
of wall art that
is inexpensive
and totally
unique

Left With a shared passion for fashion, a mother and her teenage daughter have decorated the daughter's bedroom corner with covers of Vogue magazine. Collected over the years by the mother, the covers make a fascinating piece of retro wall art.

Right Leaning against the wall, a wooden board has been covered from top to toe in a collage of images photographed during a trip to Italy. Restricting the images to letters, words, numbers, and signs, all in sharp colors, makes a unique piece of art for a teenager's bedroom.

CHAPTER 5

STORE & DISPLAY

Above An ornate Capodimonte pitcher, with a large, curved handle and a delicate body embellished with fine ceramic flowers, has been sprayed with matte black paint by its owner.

Left A collection of vintage retro china, contemporary candlesticks and candles, and other favored objects has also had the same matte black paint treatment as the pitcher above. Set against a white backdrop, they are transformed into a stunning display.

DISPLAYING COLLECTIONS

Most of us collect something. This could be very specific or quite random—it all depends on the individual. You may have a passion for photographs and choose to surround yourself with a particular style or period of photography. Or you may be fascinated by something more diverse, such as certain fabrics, shapes, or colors. Whatever you collect, every piece usually has a story to tell, and it is really important to display them all with care and in a way that will enhance your living space.

The owner of this home has collected retro vases and other objects. In their original state, they would just be a mish-mash of styles, but she had the ingenious idea of spray-painting them all in matte black. Sitting on top of the mantelpiece, where both the exposed bricks and wooden shelf are painted a stark white, her collection makes an impressive statement.

Right An impressive Indian silver decorative table holds a carefully curated selection of treasured items, from a bronze statue in the style of Rodin to a ribbed glass vase and silver boxes.

Below A plain, whitewashed table has been made to look very special simply by gathering together on it decorative items all in the same color—white.

Left Positioned precisely on the wood-paneled walls, these four silver-framed antique mirrors are spotted with age and full of character.

All-white and all-silver objects grouped together make a stylish display

Previous page A gnarled piece of an old vine has been transformed into a magnificent candle holder and now makes a bold centerpiece on a living-room table. Creating a perfect balance is the pair of metal scroll lamps with their rust finish.

Left All eyes are on the precious items displayed as the plain floating shelves seem to disappear into the white wall. Carefully arranged by material type, the objects create a soothing and intriguing arrangement.

Above These pristine white drawers allow the display of collectibles to take center stage.

The owners of this home have mastered the art of display. The rooms reflect the understanding and consideration they have given to their surroundings. Their very well-thought-out collection of global finds sits alongside objects that hold a deep significance for them, along with treasured gifts from friends. Nothing of insignificance to the couple graces the shelves and cabinets. Many pieces represent travels to exotic, far-flung places, where they have searched out the unusual to bring back home. In the living room, strong African carvings sit harmoniously alongside simple shapes of clear glass on a run of white drawers. A well-worn leather chair unifies the scheme, helping to keep the space serene and well ordered. An oriental theme dominates in the hallway.

This huge circular metal bookcase is from Anthropologie. Both striking and useful, it displays family photographs, books, with practical as well as decorative bookends, and also art. The piece of painted wood in the center is by the Italian artist Nicola Bolla.

EVERY FRIDAY

STREATHAM:
PAIR SNUB
TV SHOW'S
£240K BANKSY

Previous page These two shelves house some remarkable and very individual pieces of art from different eras, highlighting the very different styles and interests of the couple who live here. Top row, from left to right: a plaque by the British urban graffiti artist Stik of his signature stick man; mounted antique printing blocks; etchings of a dove and a more abstract bird; and an antique letter "R." Bottom row: mounted vintage gloves; an antique gilt frame; a vintage oil painting; and a mixed media framed pope by the French street artist Dran.

Right Clear acrylic boxes of different sizes, piled high in an irregular pattern, make a superb and discreet display case for a variety of treasured objects. As the boxes are easy to move around, changing their contents is quickly and simply done.

If you own
a collection of
beautiful things
that deserve special
focus, place them
on an "altar" to
show them at their
absolute best

This impressive collection of rare and valuable St Louis paperweights, all of them limited editions, has been assembled by the owner over a period of 25 years. With their intricate designs and breathtaking beauty, they are utterly deserving of prominent display. Similar to the display on the previous page, the owner devised a simple but ingenious display case using transparent acrylic dividers stacked together to create rows of cubbyholes. Each cubbyhole is the perfect size for a paperweight and, being transparent, they let the pieces speak for themselves without any distraction.

Paperweights as beautiful as these should be viewed from every possible angle in order to be fully appreciated. Here, transparent acrylic dividers have been stacked to form a virtually seamless wall of cubbyholes. Positioned inside the cubbyholes, the paperweights can be easily admired without needing to be handled. Another advantage is that the display case can be set up and dismantled in very little time.

A love of retro art from the 1960s and '70s is immediately apparent from these striking collections of ceramics and glass. By including only objects that she feels passionate about, the owner, with her focused eye for color and detail, has created two very well-curated displays.

This collection of old glass bottles takes us back to a time before the arrival of the convenient but ghastly plastic bottle that now pollutes our planet. During their lifetimes, these beautifully crafted containers have been used over and over again, with each one telling its own story.

Favorite tipples from local brasseries were sealed in by wire-sprung ceramic stoppers and rubber seals, consumed, and then recycled. Heavy green glass bottles, produced exclusively for specific vineyards and bearing unique logos and designs, are filled with the heavenly nectar that is wine. Distinctive features, such as raised lettering and bold colors, indicate medicine bottles, while the coffin-shaped bottles with angled necks were reserved for the most dangerous concoctions! Cobalt-blue bottles, favored by pharmacies and perfumers, mingle with brown and elaborate clear-glass specimens, to complete the picture.

It's easy to imagine how much pleasure or relief some of these bottles have given to various individuals over the years. What special occasion did that heavy champagne bottle celebrate and how many generations ago? Did that pharmaceutical bottle contain a remedy to ease some poor sufferer's gout? Some of the smaller bottles have a less interesting history—they have simply been dug up from the garden. Discarded long before garbage collections, their usefulness is over but they have been rediscovered as decorative memorabilia.

Left and above Tall, short, narrow, and round, bottles in all shapes, sizes, and colors sit on a windowsill in their final incarnation as decorative objects, cheering up an east-facing window. As the sun rises, the light refracts through the glass, showering the kitchen with a myriad rainbow colors.

Left and below Earthy tones prevail in the entrance hall and dining area of this home. The objects and art on display in both cases create a casual feel but have in fact been thoughtfully selected to tie in with their surroundings.

Right The apparent simplicity of this conservatory display belies how carefully it has been curated. Taking into account color, texture, and material, a simple balance has been achieved, with each object having a story to tell.

Two distinct interiors are pictured here, each displaying a keen eye for color, material, and effect. In the sun-filled conservatory, a collection of simple everyday items highlights the owner's disciplined eye and well-trained sense of style. Confidently sitting together on shelves in a seemingly casual arrangement are objects in wood, soapstone, and porcelain, complemented by dried flowers and pieces of coral. Their natural colors fuse together to produce a gentle tonal space, where the light is softened by the handmade linen shades.

WALL ART

For me, a wall is a beautiful blank canvas. A great big opportunity. My "paints" are anything I can hang or lean against the wall—photographs, art, ceramics, carvings, obscure curios discovered in bottom drawers, gorgeous objects unearthed in unlikely flea markets. What is key in creating wall art is that it should reflect you, your interests, and your personality.

The thick walls of this old cottage, high in the hills of southwest France, are showing their age gracefully. Sun-bleached summers and the passing of time have caused the plaster to peel, making unusual and unexpected patterns on the walls. The effect is quite magical, and how thrilling it is to use the patterns as part of the wall display.

A variety of individual vintage plates of different sizes, positioned so that they enhance the pattern on the worn wall, creates a flow, which makes the space very pleasing to look at and totally unique. There is something of a Dutch still-life painting about it. For this idea to work, you need to choose a color palette—in this instance, it is blue. Hang up the plates with plate hangers and overlap them, using a small block of wood to get them to stand away from the wall. The 3-D effect created in this way gives more depth to the display.

This is a very casual living space, without a hint of formality, so playing with a blank expanse of wall in this way suits the atmosphere perfectly. It's also enormous fun! If you tire of the display, something else catches your eye, or the markings on the wall change, this random piece of wall art of plates can simply and quickly be replaced by something else.

Although the sinuous pattern created by the plates looks quite random, it is actually imitating the natural markings on the plaster wall caused by the passing of time. It creates a remarkably effective decoration that transforms an otherwise ordinary wall.

What these two photos of different parts of the same large Georgian house have in common is how they make the most of the wall space and create imposing and dramatic vignettes. You are in little doubt that great care and consideration have gone into displaying treasured collections.

The owners bought the collection of antlers whole, and it now hangs with great majesty on the landing wall, illuminated by the skylight. Perched on the large carved cabinet at the top of the stairs is a glass display case containing a beautiful stuffed turkey. The forlorn-looking toy donkey, worn out by children over the generations, has a rather different history.

Within the recessed curved wall in the living room is a cleverly composed vignette. A deep-buttoned, satin-covered, high-backed chair with the splash of a red satin cushion provides glamour to the dark space. The gap left above the chair has been filled with skulls and horns of various shapes and sizes, which are positioned on the wall with pinpoint accuracy. The top of the recess creates a frame-like effect, drawing the eye to the display. Perched on a small occasional table sits a glass dome with an owl inside, peeking out at a crocodile jaw. Among all these hunting trophies stands a large, carved religious statue. This might seem a rather incongruous addition but the unexpected mix of objects does work exceedingly well.

Left The soft curve of the banister and the creaky wooden floorboards on the landing help to make this the perfect wall space for skulls and horns, the trophies of one man's hunting exploits in 1928.

Above A mix of the sacred and profane makes a surprising but very successful vignette in this living room recess. The curved arch of the recess creates a frame-like effect and draws the eye to the wall display.

Surrounding this imposing, intricately carved Victorian dresser is a very impressive selection of stuffed birds, from ducks to birds of prey, all displayed in their original boxes. Each box has a hand-painted backdrop and contains an environment appropriate to its subject, such as a piece of wood to resemble a branch. The museum-like effect is deliberate. It invites visitors to peer and inspect, as well as admire. Looking like an intrinsic part of the collection, the dresser, with its selection of crystal decanters and bottles of spirits, is the centerpiece of this reception room.

Creating a collection as impressive as this takes time, effort, patience, and research. The owners have been relentless in their quest, traveling far and wide over a number of years, to build up their collection, but it has paid dividends. They have ended up with a collection that looks as if it were tailor-made because all the birds and their boxes complement each other so well.

Right Dark and imposing, this museum-like reception room is an homage to taxidermy and invites close inspection of its resident birds and animals. Grouped together in their original boxes, the birds are truly an impressive sight.

Next page Driftwood provides the most natural art. Hanging from hooks in the wall and randomly placed, these organic forms take on a life of their own. This breathtaking display costs next to nothing to create, and is so easy to do.

Left On top of the recycled, dark-stained sideboard, vintage glass decanters and jars form part of a carefully curated selection of objects collected over the years, complementing the display of personal photographs above.

Right The large photograph of a building reflected in a puddle was taken by the homeowner. It is hung above a vintage, brushed-steel office cabinet, which doubles up as handsome storage and a display surface that is of huge interest to the owner's dog, Alfie.

displaying photographs

Photography has always provided an easy way of decorating your home, but taking time to consider colors, size, frames, and subject can work toward specifically enhancing the interior design of the room they're displayed in, as well as telling a story of your choice.

This sleek and well-thought-out display is achieved through using matching unobtrusive frames, which are uniformly sized and spaced on the wall. The look is made even more cohesive by sticking to only black-and-white photographs. The subjects of the photographs are the owner's two daughters, taken at different moments throughout their lives. The owner is a photographer and took these himself, meaning this display has even greater personal significance.

Two different homes show their precious family photographs in contrasting ways. One collection is presented in dark frames, appearing jumbled but actually very ordered, while the other is in stark, white frames, hanging in a uniform block. Displaying photographs of family over the generations is like inviting them into your home to share your daily lives.

mirror magic

Hanging in a group, a collection of convex mirrors in smooth black frames cleverly reflects its surroundings. The effect of convex mirrors can be quite disorientating, as familiar objects appear distorted, either squashed or enlarged in their reflections—the wooden chandelier in the center of the room looks especially imposing. Each mirror produces a slightly different effect, according to its size and position on the wall, resulting in an unsettling, three-dimensional feel and an illusion of greater depth in the room.

Giving a certain symmetry to the scene is a pair of decorative metal lamps with mushroom linen shades, positioned either side of the mirrors on a console table. Another convex mirror, with a plume-effect, gold-painted wooden frame, adds to the intriguing sense of drama and illusion.

When hanging mirrors, you need to consider very carefully where you position art and lamps. For maximum impact, their reflections need to create balance and a sense of order in the room. Convex mirrors need particular care, as they can distort objects almost beyond recognition. Light reflected in these mirrors takes on a more solid and diffuse appearance, so make sure you position lamps at an angle to them.

Convex mirrors of various sizes hung together create a wall of intriguing reflections, while the two decorative lamps with their linen shades add symmetry to the room. When lit, the lamps throw a soft light onto the wall, helping to achieve a warm ambiance.

By positioning mirrors strategically, you can very cleverly bring the outside into your home. Doing just that in this mountaintop retreat in the south of France has created a stunning image. Just look at the breathtaking reflection of the distant landscape in one of the antique mirrors. This setting is perfect. Art and mirrors hanging on the pale pink plaster wall sit so comfortably with the desiccated colors of the hydrangeas. The muted greens of the vintage glass flagons, along with the books, add to the harmony. When combined, mirrors and lights are a tour de force. The double image of the crystal chandelier contributes to the three-dimensional effect and it is even more striking at night.

Left Mirrors and art share this wall space. Perfectly married to the sun-bleached look of the room, the mirrors gently reflect the region and all that's special about it. The overall image is one of peace and tranquility.

Next page A sense of drama is achieved in this hallway with vintage mirrors lining every wall. The effect is disorientating, and it is difficult to fathom the shape and size of the room and where the light is coming from.

Left A rather dark hallway lends itself perfectly to this leaning art. Bespoke open-fronted cupboards, built expressly for collections of magazines, are the perfect platform for leaning pictures in a narrow space. The pictures are easy to move around, simple to clean, and totally interchangeable.

Right Choosing similar frames and a common theme—portraits of friends and family, photos, and charcoal sketches—allows you to layer in new acquisitions. Crop pictures with others to accentuate certain characteristics, such as the surprised eyes of this self-portrait.

CREATIVE STORAGE

Finding enough space in your home to keep all your possessions is a dilemma for many of us, but with a little thought, you can create storage in your home and even use it to add character to rooms.

In this hallway in my own home, two collections are stored: magazines and framed art. Open-fronted cupboards such as these provide a fantastic way of combining storage and display—in effect, they are a large-scale version of the transparent acrylic dividers on pages 218–219. You could easily vary the content of each cupboard for a more varied look, or keep them all the same, as I have done.

The cupboards also provide space for a careful arrangement of the pictures leaning on top of them. Big pictures sit behind small ones, allowing each the opportunity to be exposed. The common color theme of black and white helps create a unified look. Leaning art is also flexible—you can give a different picture center stage whenever you want.

A low bookcase runs the length of one living room wall to hold a large number of books, plus CDs and a stereo, while also allowing the splendid double doors with all their original moldings to remain unshadowed. Balancing the display at either end is a ceramic peacock from 1928 and a bronze statue by Gustave Miklos.

The focus of this picture is the high-gloss, tangerine-colored strip wall cabinet. Although it is functional, concealing DVDs and books behind its doors and also acting as a shelf, its purpose is primarily that of decoration, as a piece of wall art.

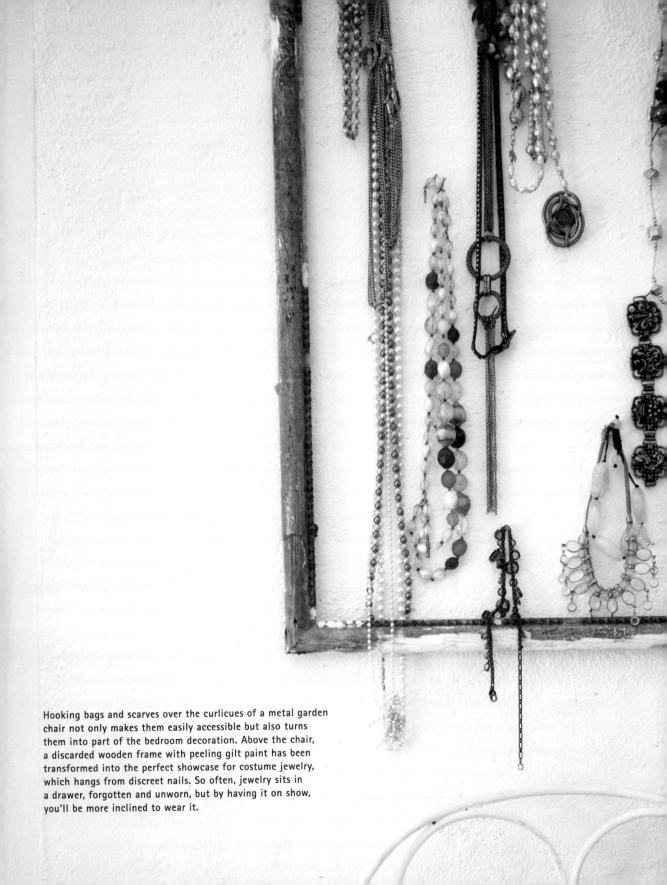

Hooking bags and scarves over the curlicues of a metal garden chair not only makes them easily accessible but also turns them into part of the bedroom decoration. Above the chair, a discarded wooden frame with peeling gilt paint has been transformed into the perfect showcase for costume jewelry, which hangs from discreet nails. So often, jewelry sits in a drawer, forgotten and unworn, but by having it on show, you'll be more inclined to wear it.

Transform your collection of bags into easily accessible art

You'd be hard pressed to find a woman who doesn't have a collection of bags and baskets that she loves, but so often a newer model comes along and the old favorites become forgotten and neglected, stored away out of sight in a closet.

Like photographs, the bags here bring back memories. They recall a time, an occasion, a vacation, a wedding, even a child's face when young! So, to acknowledge their significance, the bags have become art. Hanging from hooks on a vintage painted shelf, they are on show, to be admired but also ready to be used. Their colors and patterns sit together seamlessly, creating an unusual and practical work of art for the bedroom.

Left and right A vintage painted shelf has been devoted to a collection of bags that, between them, hold memories of many special occasions. Not only do they enhance the space, they are also conveniently close to hand.

INDEX

Page numbers in *italics* refer to illustrations

A

Alexander, Peter 49
Alvarez, Aurelie *118*
Amélie, Laurence *86*
Andreesen, Rainer *30*
Andrew, Lisa *163*
Anglepoise lamp *173*
Anthropologie *213*
artistic spaces 122–35
artwork 226–37
  in bathrooms *190*, 191
  in bedrooms 148, *148–9*, *194*, 196, 252, *252*, *253*
  in dining rooms 28, *50–1*
  in home offices 114, *118–19*, 124, *134–5*, *176*
  in kitchens *12*
  in living areas 74, *86–95*, *240–1*, *241*, *244*, 245, *245*, *248–9*
  outdoor 65

B

bags, displaying 250, 252, *252*, *253*
Bailey, David *75*
basins 182, *183*, *193*
bathrooms 182–93
bathtubs 184, *185*, 188, *193*
Bauhaus 151
bed linen 148, 160, *161*, *164–5*, 169
bedrooms 146–201
  artwork in 252, *252*, *253*
  children's rooms 194–201
  guest bedrooms 168, *169*, *171*, 186, *192–3*
  master bedrooms 148, *164–5*, 168, 180, *180*
  using display in 166–71
blinds 33, *55*, *173*
Bolla, Nicola *213*
bookshelves *106–9*, *212–13*, *246–7*
bottles *185*, *186*, *222*, 223, *223*
Broadhurst, Florence *163*

C

cabinets: bedroom *155*, *173*
  dining room *29*
  display 229
  industrial 35

kitchen *44–5*
living room *211*, *248–9*
office 235
candles 39, *41*, *59*, *76–7*, *175*, 188
  candle holders *61*, *120*, *168*, 169, *204*, 208–9
Cappellini *54*
chairs 250
  antique *42–3*, *74*, *75*, *96*, *158*, *162*, *211*
  armchairs 23, *94–5*, *104*, *106–7*, 229
  bathroom *184*
  Danish Modern *103*
  dining *30*, *52–3*
  Eero Saarinen *44–5*
  Lloyd Loom 65
  office 23
  outdoor 62, *63*
  Probber club chair 98
  Tom Charnock 49
chalkboards 196, *198*
chandeliers *156–7*, *187*, *198*, 241
  over tables *12–13*, *29*, *38–9*, *41*, 49
Charnock, Tom 49
chest-of-drawers *147*
chests *178*
children's rooms 194–201
Cire Trudon *186*
clocks 15, *16*, *96*
collections, displaying *18–22*, *31*, *64*, 65, *65*, *138–9*, 205–53
Colombo, Joe *185*
color schemes: accent colors *72*, *88–9*, *96*, *102*, *114*
  blue and white 56
  cream *166–7*
  dark colors 102
  monochrome 17, 114, *150–1*, 179, *204*, 205
  neutrals *97*, 155, *180*
  warm color palettes *152–3*
  white *46–7*, *68–9*, 69, 72, 146, 184
commodes *179*
conservatories *225*
cupboards: bathroom *193*
  bedroom *168*
  kitchen *10–11*, 11, 16
  hall *244*, 245
curtains *162–3*, 182

D

Dalton, Andrew *31*
Danish Modern *103*
Davies, Philip *95*
Denby *106–7*

Derian, John *96*
desks 123, *126*, 127, *128*, 133
Detiger, Jonny 53
dining 22–65
Diptyque *175*
displays 202–53
  in bathrooms *185*, 186, *186*, *188*
  in bedrooms 166–71
  in living rooms 86–93
doors 160, *198*
  recycled as tables *84*, 85, *85*
Dran *75*, *214–15*
drawers 211, *211*
dressers 230
dressing tables *177*
driftwood *232–3*
D'Vatz, Timu 49

E

Eames, Charles and Ray *54–5*
Egan, Andrew *103*
Emin, Tracey 28
Ercole 58, 168, *168*

F

fabric, retro-style 94
fashion designers 136–43
filing cabinets 172, *173*
fireplaces 72, *73*, 77
flooring: flagstone 84
  wooden floors 28, 35, *68–9*, *98–9*, *156*, 159, *193*, *229*
Flos *175*
flowers 14, 28, *43*, *45*, 48, *61*, 123
footstools 83, *83*
Fornasetti *108–9*
Franceschini, Ubaldo *86*
furniture: bedside 172–81
  see also chairs; tables, *etc*

G

G Plan *106–7*
Gibson, Natalie *106*

H

hallways *244*, 245
headboards *164–5*, *179*, 180
Hirst, Damien *140–1*
Holt, Liddy *102*
home offices 112–19
Hornsea *106–7*

J

Jeré, Curtis *164*, *187*
jewelry 250, *251*

K

kitchens 11–27, *44–5*

L

landings *160*
Le Klint *172*
letters 198, *199*
libraries *108–9*
lighting: antique lamps *121, 147, 151*
  bathroom *185*
  bedroom *147, 148, 151, 156–7, 159, 160, 166, 169, 172, 173, 175, 176, 177,* 198
  candlelight *38–9, 59, 61, 76–7*
  chandeliers *12–13, 29, 38–9, 41,* 49, *156–7, 187,* 198, *241*
  desk lamps *80, 132*
  floor lamps 94, *98, 103, 175*
  industrial lighting *32, 160*
  natural *171, 171, 186, 223*
  pea lights *100–1*
  pendant lights *14,* 97, *172, 172*
  table lamps *72,* 74, 79, *79, 80, 92, 114, 126, 159, 208–9, 239*
Ling, David 53
living spaces, creative 68–109
Lloyd Loom 65
luggage racks 188, *188–9, 191*

M

magazine racks *147*
memory boards *116–17*
metal signs 155
Miklos, Gustave *247*
mirrors: in bathrooms *187*
  in bedrooms 148, *177,* 180
  in dining areas *28, 40–1*
  in living areas *90, 92,* 206
  in home offices *136, 143*
  as wall art *88–9, 238–43*
modern retro 94–109
murals *152–3*

N

Nelson, George *98*
nightstands *154, 157, 159, 166,* 168, *169, 171, 174, 175, 176, 177, 179*
Nott, Richard *28, 247*
numbers, vintage *16,* 17, *17*

O

offices, home 112–19
oriental designs *42–3*
Oschmann, Leslie *119*

ottomans *76–7*
outdoor dining 56–65

P

packing crates *82,* 83
photographs 170, 171, *194–6,* 205, *234–7*
pinboards *112, 113, 121*
Pitfield London *106–7*
place cards 63, *63*
plate racks 19
plates *64,* 65, *65,* 226, *226–7*
postcard collections 124, *124–5*
Probber, Harvey 98

R

radiators *149, 158*
recycling materials 81–5
Reeves, Michael *179*
rugs *54–5,* 72, 97

S

Saarinen, Eero *44–5, 72, 151, 175*
scarves *250*
screening rooms *106–7*
screens *42–3, 71, 79, 179*
seashells 188, *191*
Secot Design 97
shelving: bookshelves *106–7, 108–9, 212–13, 246–7*
  home office 129, *143*
  storage and display 11, *210, 214–19,* 224, *248–9*
shutters *74,* 97, 148, *154, 156,* 171
sideboards 234
sofas *22,* 54, *69, 75, 90,* 97, *98, 102, 105*
Spode teapot *43*
Starck, Philippe *184*
Stik *214*
stools *173*
storage 202–25, 244–53
  bathroom 182, *185,* 188, *188–9, 191,* 193
  bedroom *172*
  kitchen 11, 15, *15, 19, 20–1*
studios 120–43

T

tables: art tables *120, 121,* 123
  bathroom *184*
  bedside *see* nightstand
  coffee *79, 81, 82,* 83, *83, 84–5,* 98, *107, 109*
  console *31*

dining *14, 29, 30, 33, 34, 36–9, 43, 44, 46–7,* 49, *52–3,* 53, *54–5*
  dressing *177, 193*
  Ercole *58*
  garden *79*
  home office *114,* 137
  kitchen *12–13,* 15
  lacquered *43*
  living room *208–9*
  marble-topped *54–5*
  metal *26–7, 34,* 35
  nightstand *154, 157, 159, 166,* 168, *169, 171, 174, 175, 176, 177, 179*
  occasional 78–85, *91, 96, 206, 207,* 229
  outdoor 57, *62, 63*
  Plexiglass *52–3,* 53
  Saarinen *72, 151, 175*
  side tables *80,* 94, *94*
  table settings 22, *22–7, 30,* 31, *32, 36–9, 43*
  wooden *30, 31, 32, 44–5,* 48, *52–3,* 53, *61*
taxidermy *230–1*
teenage bedrooms 198
texture, adding *88–9*
Thompson, Martyn 98
throws *88–9,* 91, 180
tiles: floor *185*
  wall 11, *185,* 186, *187,* 188, 190
Tita, Fabius *126*
toile de Jouy *177*
trunks 83, *83*

V

Villiers, Henry *192*
Viramontes, Tony 87, *87*

W

wall sconces *59*
wallpaper *71, 168, 174*
walls: brick *73,* 98, *98–9*
  concrete *183*
  tiled 11, *185,* 186, *187,* 188, 190
  wood-paneled *116–17, 124–5,* 160, *164–5, 193, 206*
Warhol, Andy 54
washstands 168, *168*
Wells, Ebert *103*
Woodard, Russell *30*
work spaces 110–43

PICTURE CREDITS

Abigail Aked (www.abigailaked.co.uk): pages 128–129

Laurence Amélie and Ubaldo Franceschini (www.laurence-amelie. com) (www.ubaldo-franceschini. blogspot.com): pages 12–13, 123

Kyle Andrew: pages 88–89, 162–163

Lily Ashwell (www.lilyashwell.com): pages 136–137

Rachel Ashwell (www.rachelashwellshabbychiccouture. com): pages 36–37, 56–57, 67, 79 top middle, 86, 112–113, 177 right

Joel Bernstein (www.cocomaya.co.uk): pages 10–11, 160–161, 192–193

Kris Bones: pages 154–155

Paul Brewster and Shaun Clarkson (www.pitfieldlondon.com): pages 106–107, 164–165, 187

Nicky Butler: pages 49, 87, 246–247

Oana Camilleri (www.oanacamilleri. blogspot.com): pages 130–131

Lisa Carrier: pages 120–121

Marie-France Cohen (www.merci-merci.com): pages 11, 14–15, 83

Paul and Tina Curtin: pages 38–39, 60–61, 62–63, 84–85, 116–117, 177 left, 203, 207 bottom, 222–223, 226–227, 232–233, 240–241, 242–243, 250–251

Lee Curtis: pages 134–135

Marilyn and Julyan Day: pages 24–25, 26–27, 76–77, 78, 152–153, 176 left, 208–209

John Derian (www.johnderian.com): pages 90–91, 92–93, 144, 156–157, 158–159

John Derian Store, NYC: pages 238–239

The Detiger family (www.jonnydetiger. com): pages 52 top, 53 top, 82

Andrew Egan: pages 16–17, 50–51, 104–105, 114–115

Zoe Ellison: pages 166–167, 225, 236

Robert Falconer: pages 216–217

Barnaba Fornasetti (www.fornasetti.com): pages 108–109, 126–127

Gisela Garcia-Escuela: pages 66, 73, 118–119, 212–213

Emma Gibson (www.egibson.co.uk): page 133 left and middle

Trevor Halls and Mark Cooke: page 176 right

Liddie and Howard Harrison (www.holtharrison.co.uk): pages 18–19, 81, 188–189, 190–191, 228–229, 230–231

Tim Hartley: pages 54–55, 150–151, 175, 185, 186

Rick and Debra Haylor (www.rickhaylor.com): pages 34–35, 234–235, cover spine

Christine Innamorato: pages 110, 122

Betty Jackson and David Cohen: pages 94–95, 182–183

Geraldine James: pages 10, 20–21, 28–29, 64–65, 79 bottom left, 202, 244–245, 252–253

Michael Johnston: pages 218–219

Alex Legendre: pages 198–199, 224

Mick Lindberg and Arun Soni: pages 138–139

Kit and Max Li-Perry: pages 172–173

Fran Macmillan (www.metroclapham.com): page 48

Michele Matthewman: page 52 bottom

Caitlin McCann and Bradley Ridge: pages 74–75, 214–215, front cover

Created by **Steven McFee**: page 201

Karen Murray: pages 220–221

Richard Nott and Graham Fraser (www.richardnott-artist.com): pages 3, 5, 6–7, 22–23, 124–125, 148–149, 170–171, 210–211

Ornella Pisano and Pietro Russino (www.ercolehome.com): pages 58–59, 168–169

Katie and Gino da'Prato: pages 68–69, 70–71, 145, 184

Michael Reeves (www.michaelreevesassociates.co.uk): pages 42–43, 79 top right, 178, 179 right, 207 top

David Richardson and Debbie Murphy: pages 174, 248–249

Anne and Peter Rivett: pages 2, 40–41, 46–47, 180–181, 206

Ron and Stacy Robinson: page 179

George and Diana Sharp: pages 1, 4, 30–31, 32–33, 98–99, 100–101, 102–103, 146–147, 204–205, back cover

Patrick and Christina Shaw (www.patricshawbeauty.com): pages 44–45, 72

Evie Slingsby: pages 194–195, 196–197

Nick and Anne-Marie Slingsby: page 237

Alex Starck: pages 132, 133 right

Adam Towner (www.thedeaddollsclub. com): page 80

Ian Wallace: pages 111, 140–141, 142–143

David Walker-Smith and Martin McCarthy: pages 96–97